# FOREWORD

*Yuletide Favorites* has been a barbershop holiday staple for more than three dec its tradition, *Yuletide Favorites, Vol. II* has been created as a worthy companior featuring accessible holiday arrangements in the barbershop style from Don Grimmer, Joe Johnson, Joe Liles, Greg Lyne, Adam Scott, Burt Szabo, Jeff Taylor, and Larry Triplett.

Whether caroling with a quartet or building a holiday program for your chorus, this collection offers 14 tried and true arrangements that require minimal to no rehearsal time and are easy and fun to sing. Part-specific learning tracks have been created as well as a separate full-mix listening recording to assist in learning these songs quickly and accurately.

We hope this collection enhances your enjoyment of the season and from all of us at the Barbershop Harmony Society: Happy Holidays!



Questions about the contest suitability of any song/arrangement in this collection should be directed to the judging community and measured against current contest rules. Ask *before* you sing!

We have attempted to identify sources of both words and music for each title in this collection, often written many years apart. The dates under individual song titles refer to either the first appearance of the words and music or to the first publication of the complete song.

**Editor's Note: Special thanks to Adam Scott for initiating this project during his tenure as BHS Publications Manager, and for carefully and thoughtfully assembling many of the titles featured in this collection.**


110 Seventh Avenue North, Nashville, TN 37023-3704
www.barbershop.org

JOY TO THE WORLD!
(1742, 1833)
Words by
ISAAC WATTS
Music by
GEORGE F. HANDEL
Arranged by Joe Liles
Intro Joyfully!
(Optional: on repeat go directly to key of E♭)
Tenor
Lead
Bari
Bass
Joy! Joy! Joy! Joy! Joy! Joy!
Joy! Joy! Joy! Joy!
Verses
1. Joy to the world, the Lord is come. Let earth re - ceive her King. Let ev - 'ry heart pre - pare Him room, and
2. He rules the world with truth and grace, and makes the na - tions prove the glo - ries of his right - eous - ness, and

17 18 19 20
heav'n and na - ture sing, and heav'n and na - ture sing, and
won - ders of His love, and won - ders of his love, and
1. and heav'n and na - ture sing,
2. and won - ders of His love,
1. sing, and heav'n and na - ture
2. love and won - ders of His
21 22 23 24
1.
(to ms. 1)
(Opt. to E♭)
heav'n, and heav'n and na - ture sing.
won - ders, won - ders
sing, and
love and
2.
Tag
25 26 27 28 29
Joy,
of his love.
Joy
Joy,
Joy, joy,
joy to the world, to the world!
30 31 32 33 34
to the world!
joy to the world, to the world!
joy to the world!

# DECK THE HALLS

**(1862)**

Old Welsh Air

*Arranged by Burt Szabo*

Yule - tide car - ol, fa la la la la la la la la.
Chorus 2
See the blaz - ing Yule be - fore us, fa la la la la la la la la.
Strike the harp and join the chor - us, fa la la la la la la la la.
Fol - low me in mer - ry meas - ure, fa la la la la la la la la.
While I tell of Yule - tide treas - ure, fa fa la la la la la la.
fa la la la la la

Chorus 3
Fast a-way the old year pass-es fa la la la la la la la la.
Hail the new, ye lads and lass-es, fa la la la la la la la la.
Sing we joy-ous all to-geth-er, fa la la la la la la la la.
Sing we now, la la la
la la la
Heed-less of the wind and weath-er, fa la la la la la
molto rit.
la la la la fa la la la la la la la la

# GO, TELL IT ON THE MOUNTAIN

**(1907)**

Words by
JOHN WORK, JR.

Traditional Spiritual
*Arranged by Joe Johnson*

*Lively*
**Chorus**

Tenor
Lead

Bari
Bass

Go, tell it on the moun - tain, O - ver the hills and ev - 'ry - where;

*rit.* *(last time only)*

*Fine* *(sing cues last time only)*

Go, tell it on the moun - tain That Je - sus Christ is born!

**Verses**

1. While shep - herds kept their watch - ing O'er si - lent flocks by night,
2. The shep - herds feared and trem - bled When lo! a - bove the earth
3. Down in a low - ly man - ger The hum - ble Christ was born,

Be - hold! thro' - out the heav - ens There shone a ho - ly light.
Rang out the an - gels' cho - rus That hailed the Sav - ior's birth.
And God sent us sal - va - tion That bless - ed Christ - mas morn.

*(to ms. 1)*

# THE FIRST NOEL
**(1833)**

Traditional English Carol
*Arranged by Wayne M. Grimmer*

*With exaltation*

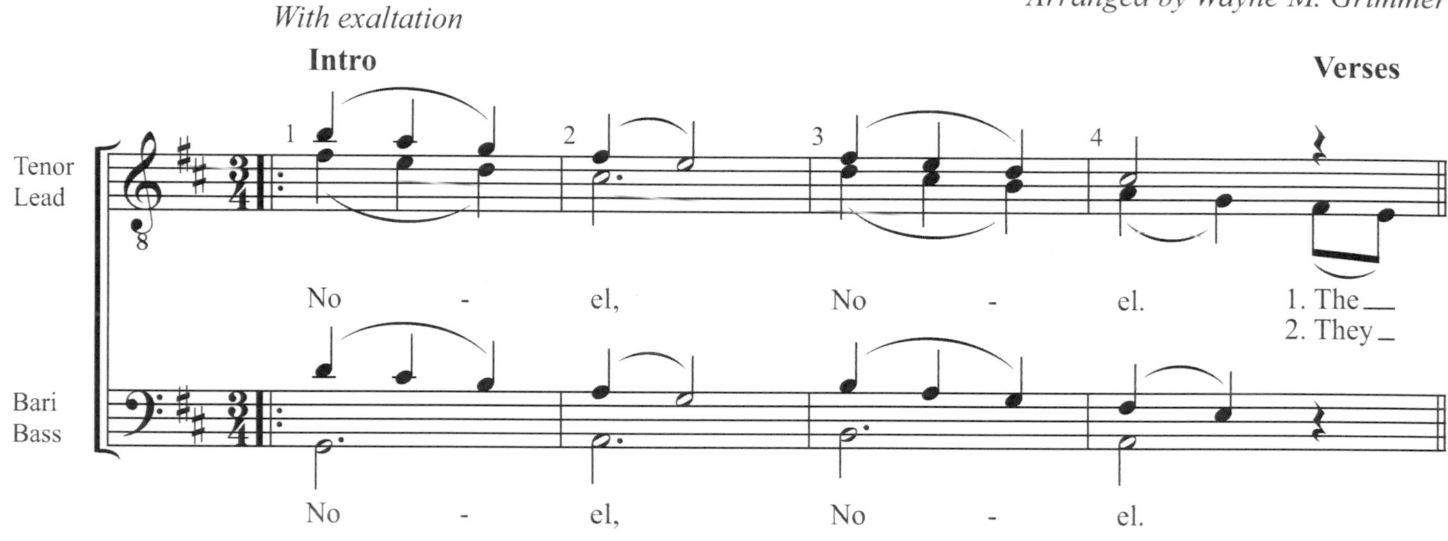


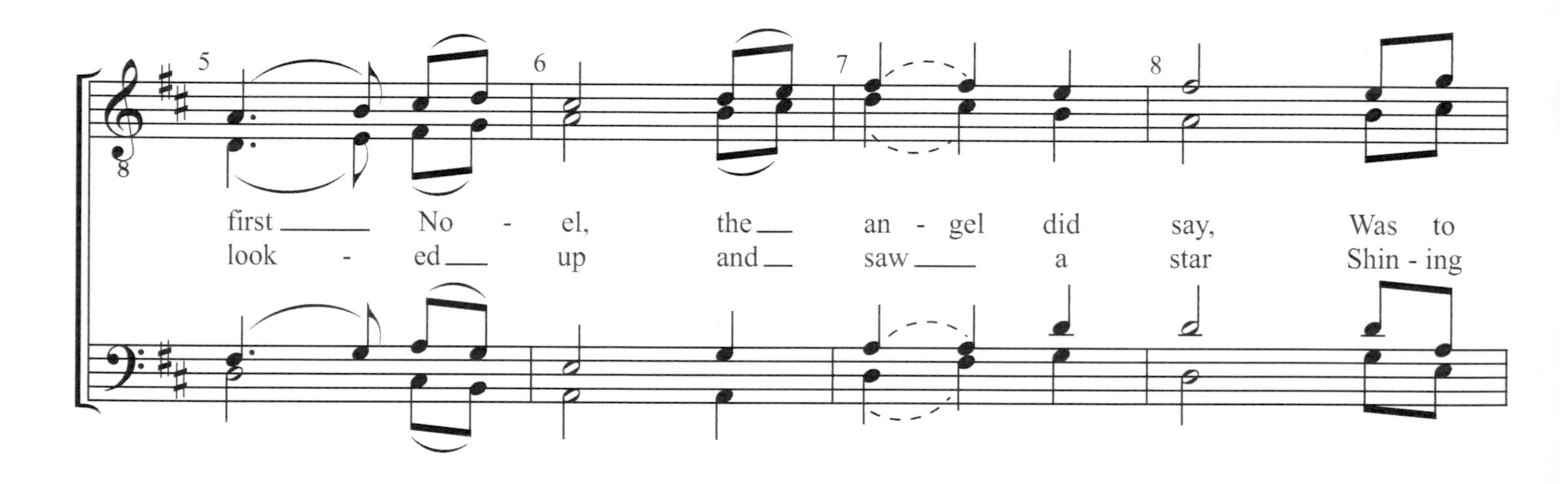

fields where they lay keep - ing their sheep, On a
to the earth, it gave great light, And
Chorus
cold win - ter's night that was so deep.
so it con - tin - ued both day and night.
No -
el, No - el, No - el, No - el,
1st time: to ms. 1
2nd time: to Tag
Born is the King of Is - ra - el.
Tag freely
Born is the King of Is - ra - el.

# GOOD CHRISTIAN MEN, REJOICE

**(1853)**

Words from Traditional Latin Carol;
Translated by JOHN M. NEALE

Traditional German Melody
*Arranged by Joe Johnson*

# WE THREE KINGS OF ORIENT ARE

# INFANT HOLY, INFANT LOWLY

**(1908)**

Translated by
EDITH M. G. REED

Traditional Polish Carol
*Arranged by Burt Szabo*

(to ms. 1)
bring - ing: Christ, the Babe, is Lord of all! 2. Flocks were

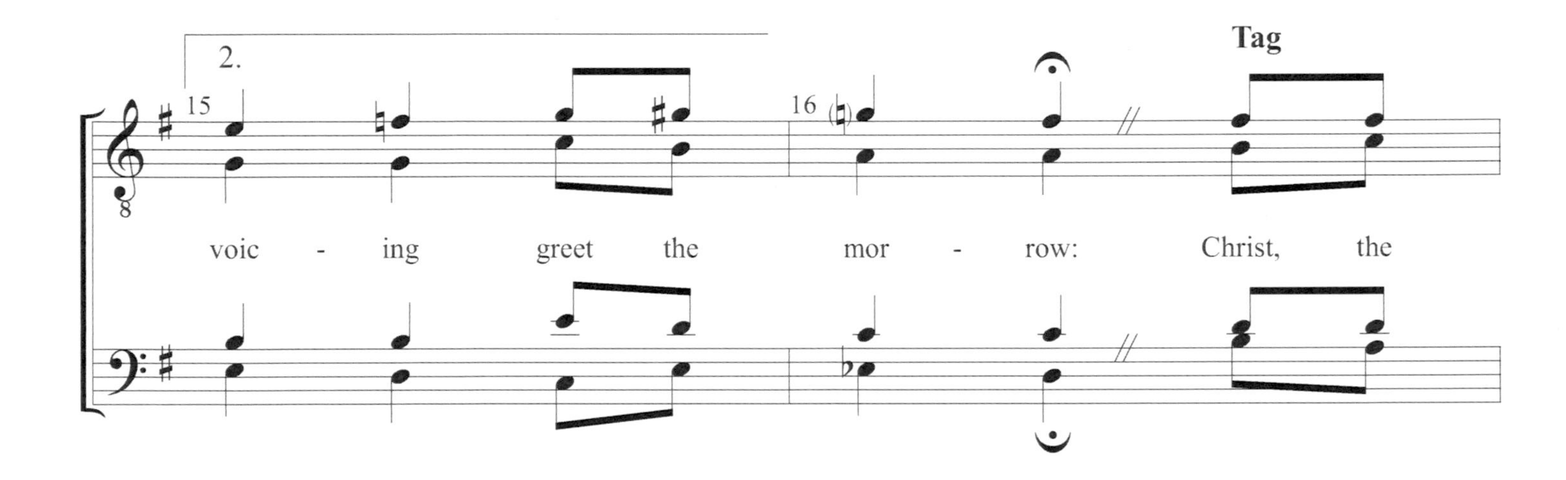
2.
Tag
voic - ing greet the mor - row: Christ, the

you! A - men, a - men.
Babe, was born for you! A - men.
you! A - men, a - men.

# WHAT CHILD IS THIS?

**(1865)**

Words by
WILLIAM C. DIX

Traditional English Melody
*Arranged by Burt Szabo*

*Optional: Baritone sing D instead of Bb

# COME, THOU LONG-EXPECTED JESUS

**(1744)**

Words by
CHARLES WESLEY

Music by
ROWLAND PRICHARD
*Arranged by Adam Scott*

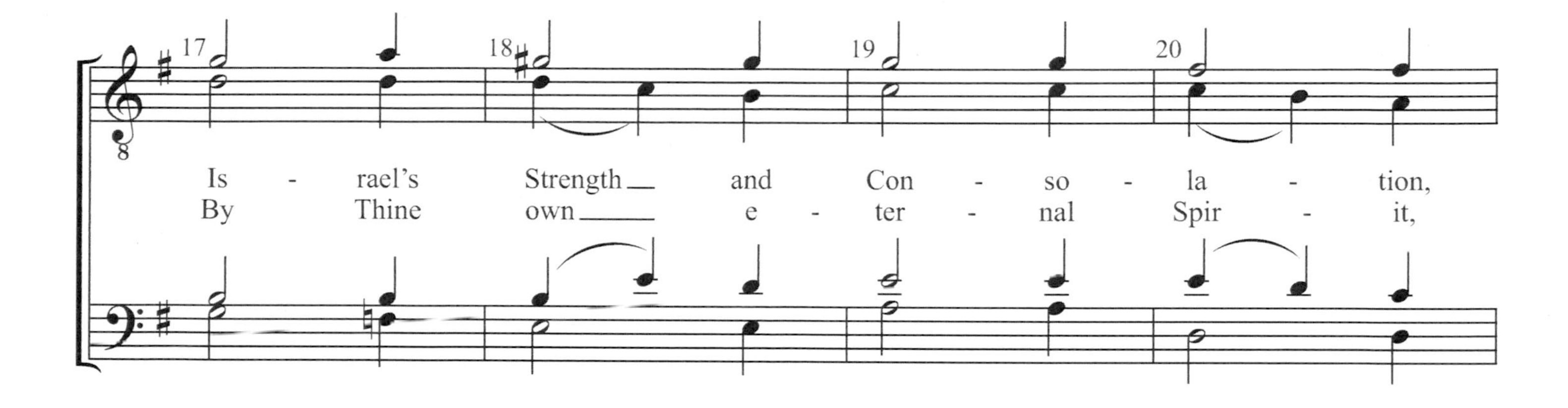
17
18
19
20
Is - rael's Strength and Con - so - la - tion,
By Thine own e - ter - nal Spir - it,

21
22
23
24
Hope of all the earth Thou art;
Rule in all our hearts a - lone;

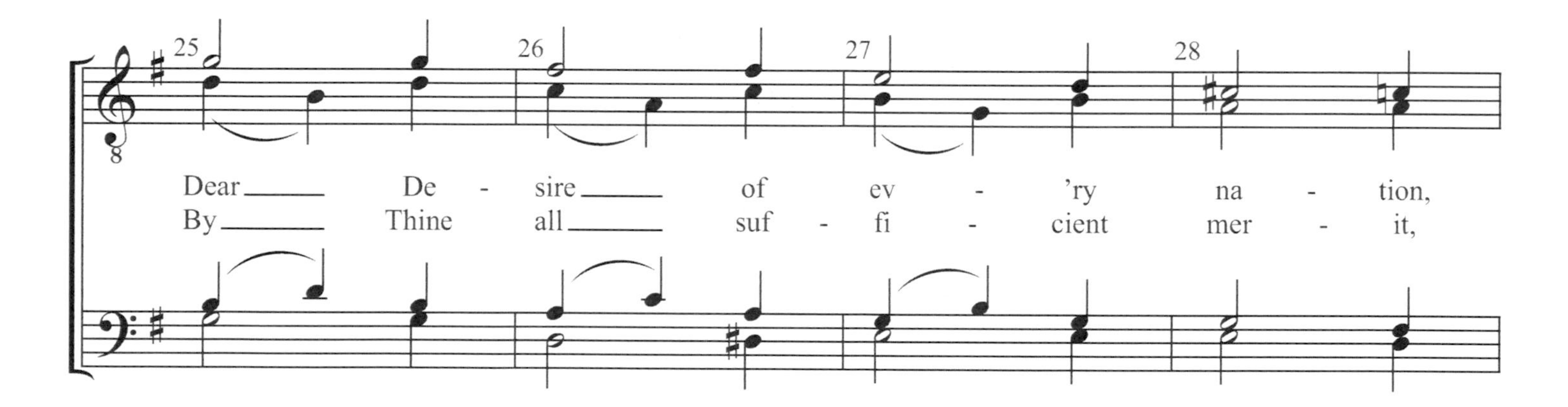
25
26
27
28
Dear De - sire of ev - 'ry na - tion,
By Thine all suf - fi - cient mer - it,

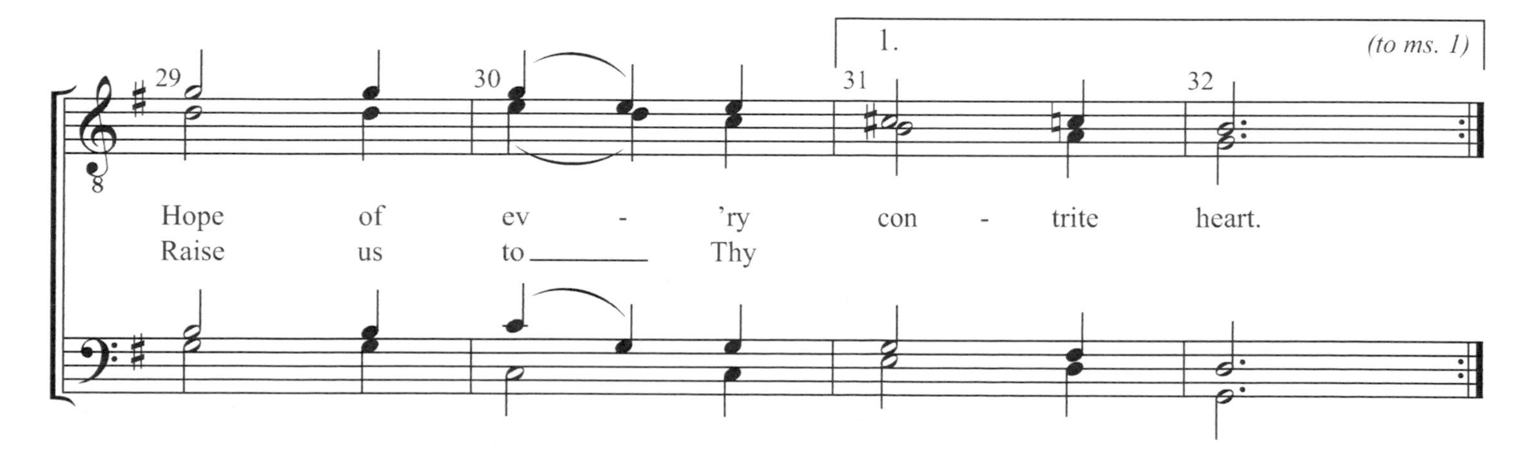
1.
(to ms. 1)
29
30
31
32
Hope of ev - 'ry con - trite heart.
Raise us to Thy

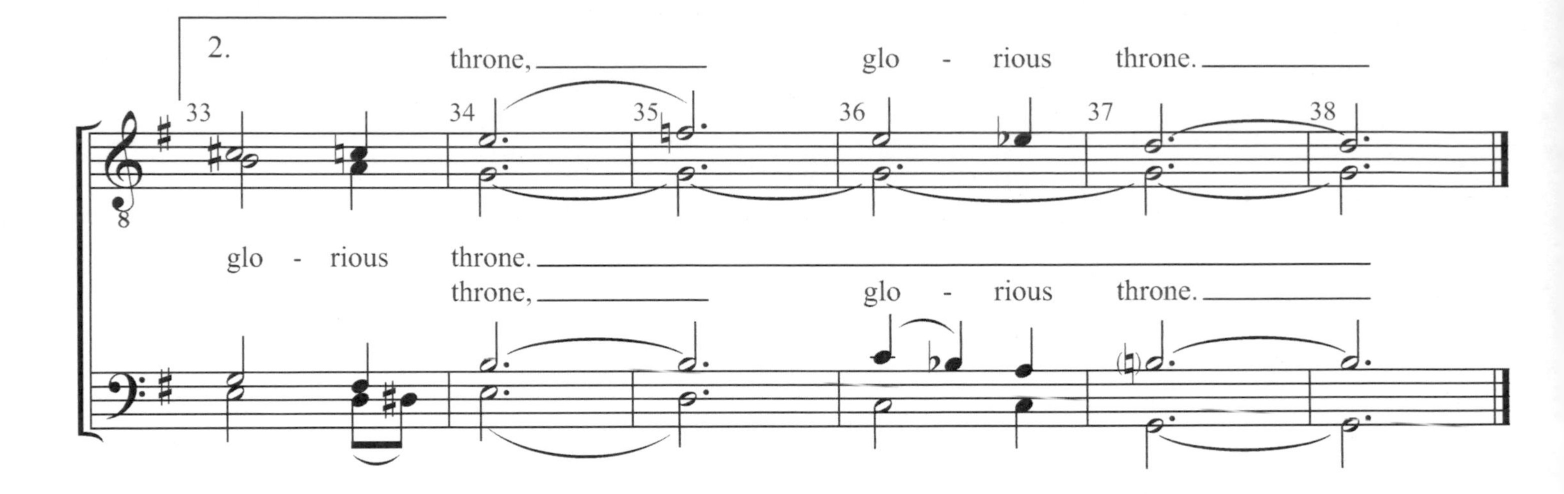


# IN THE BLEAK MIDWINTER

**(1906)**

Words by
CHRISTINA ROSSETTI

Music by
GUSTAV HOLST
*Arranged by Burt Szabo*

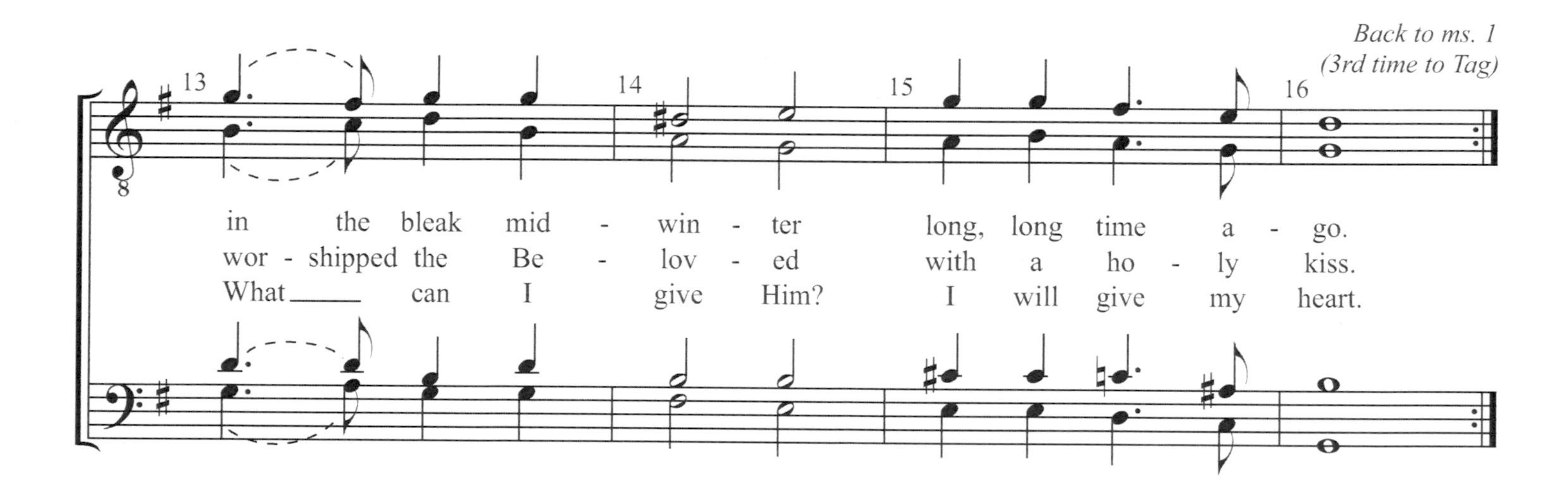


**Tag**

17 18 19

I will give ___ my heart.

# HERE WE COME A-WASSAILING

**(1850)**

Traditional English Carol
*Arranged by Larry Triplett*

12
13
14
15
too; And God bless you and send you a Hap - py New
1.
(to ms. 1)
16
17
18
19
20
Year, and God send you a Hap - py New Year.
2. We
2.
21
22
23
24
send you a Hap - py New
Year, be of good cheer!
25
26
27
28
Year!
Year, be of good cheer!

# LET ALL MORTAL FLESH KEEP SILENCE

**(1906)**

Words from the *Liturgy of St. James*;
Translated by GERARD MOULTRIE

Traditional French Carol
*Arranged by Jeff Taylor*

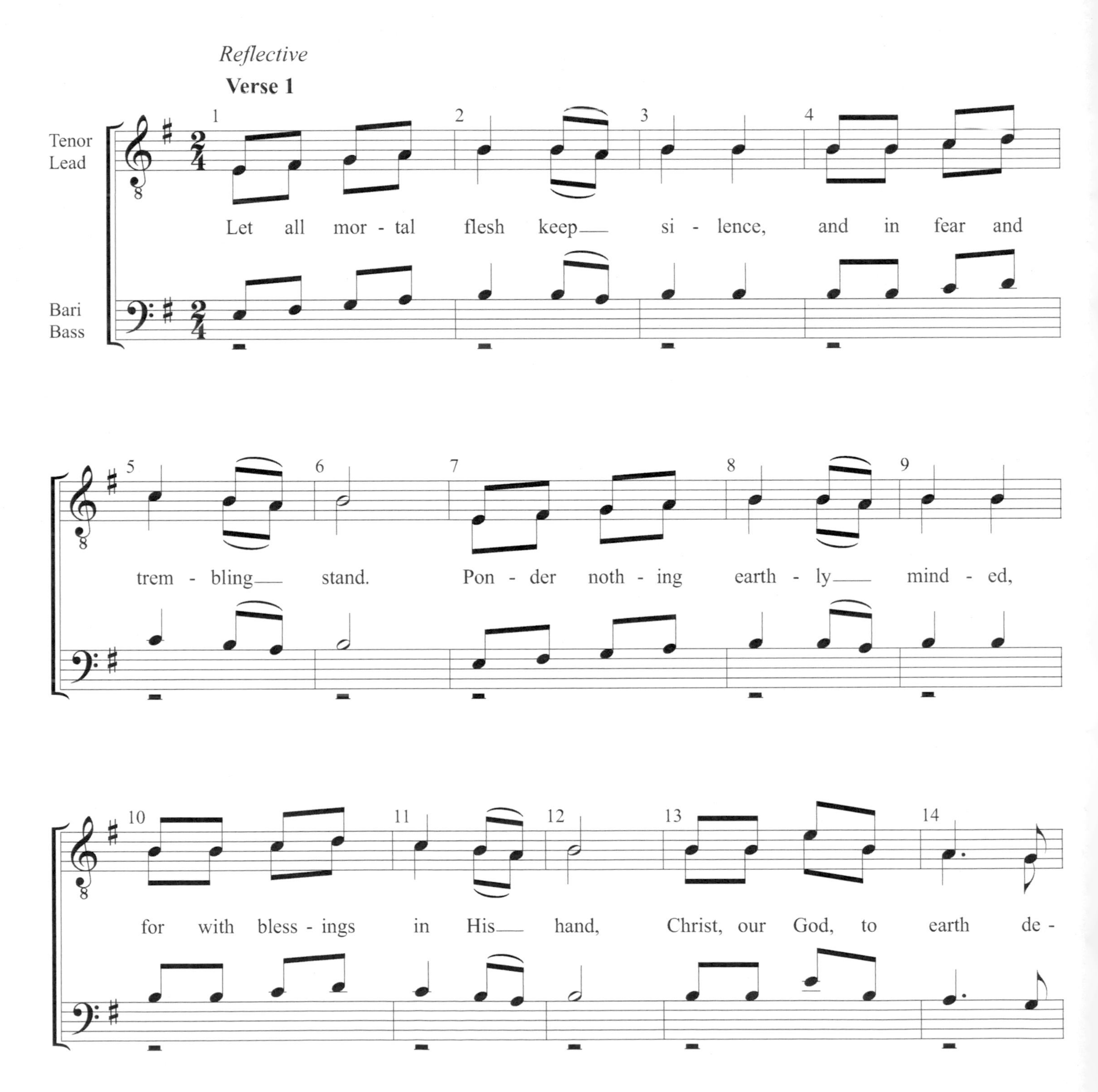

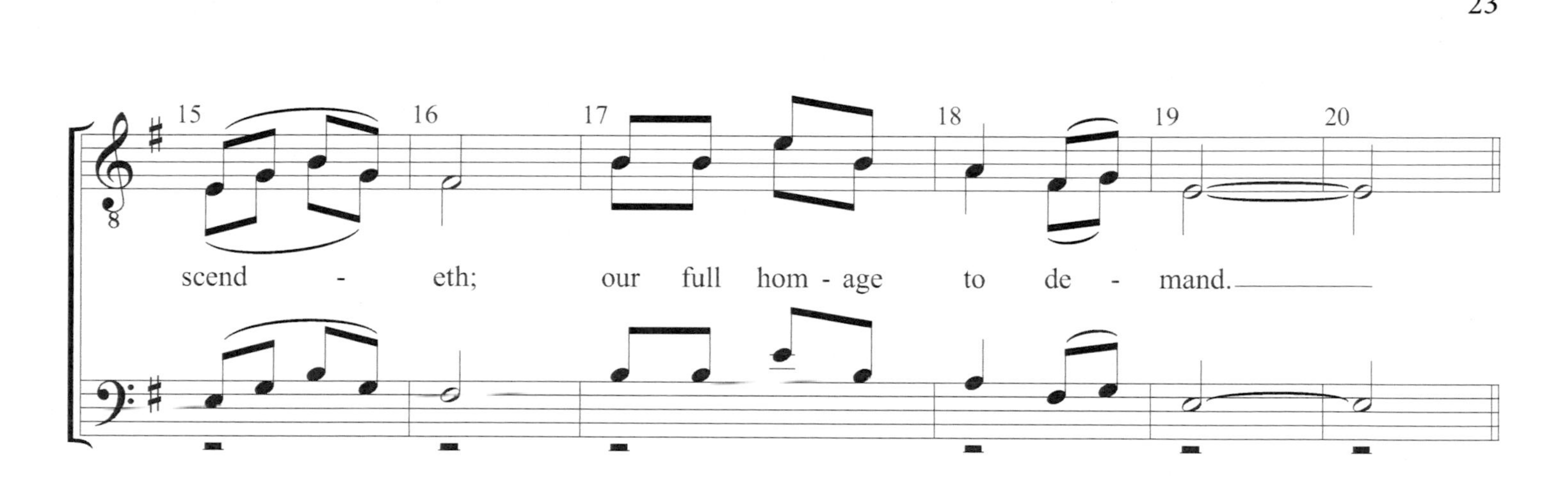
15
16
17
18
19
20
scend - eth; our full hom - age to de - mand.

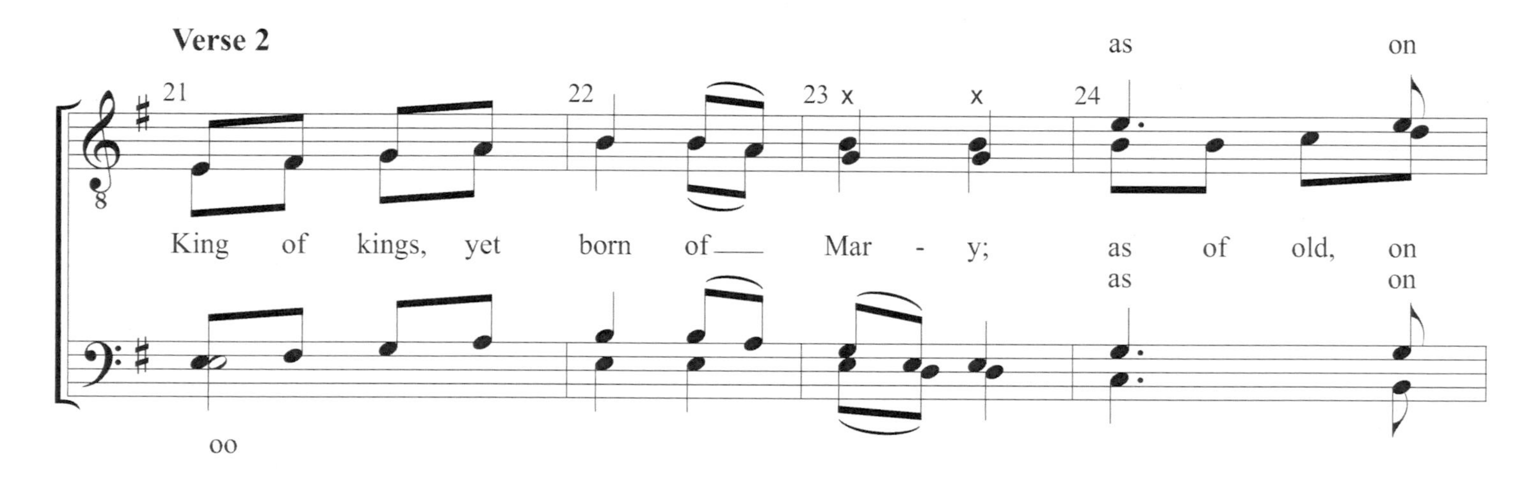
Verse 2
21
22
23
24
as on
King of kings, yet born of Mar - y; as of old, on
as on
oo

25
26
27
28
earth He stood. Lord of lords, in hu - man

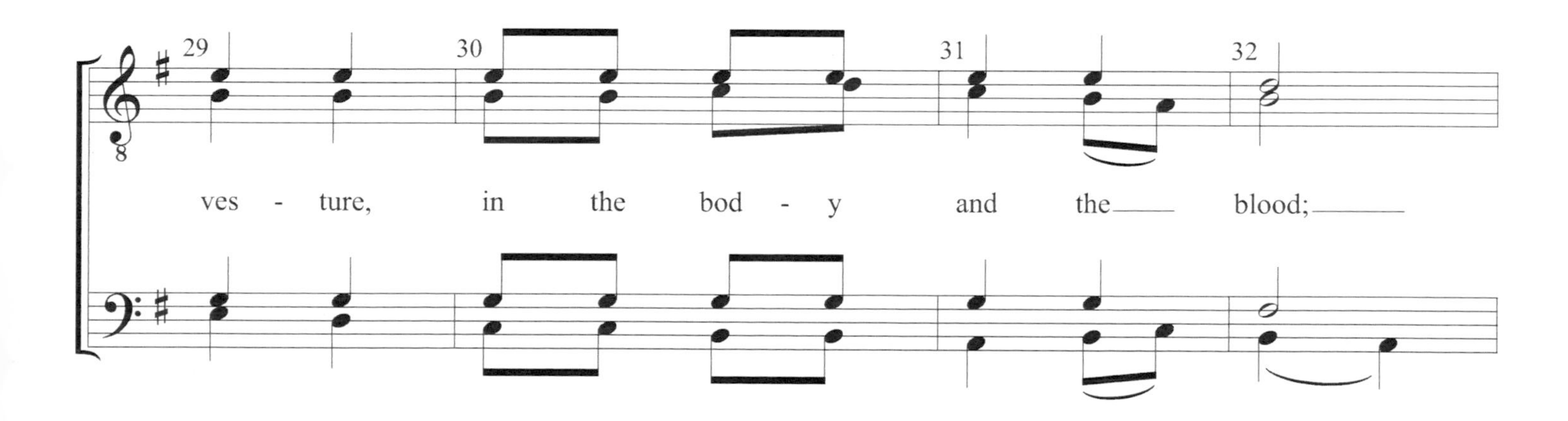
29
30
31
32
ves - ture, in the bod - y and the blood;

oo
He will give to all the faith - ful,
oo all the

oo
His own self for heav'n - ly food.
oo

**Verse 3**

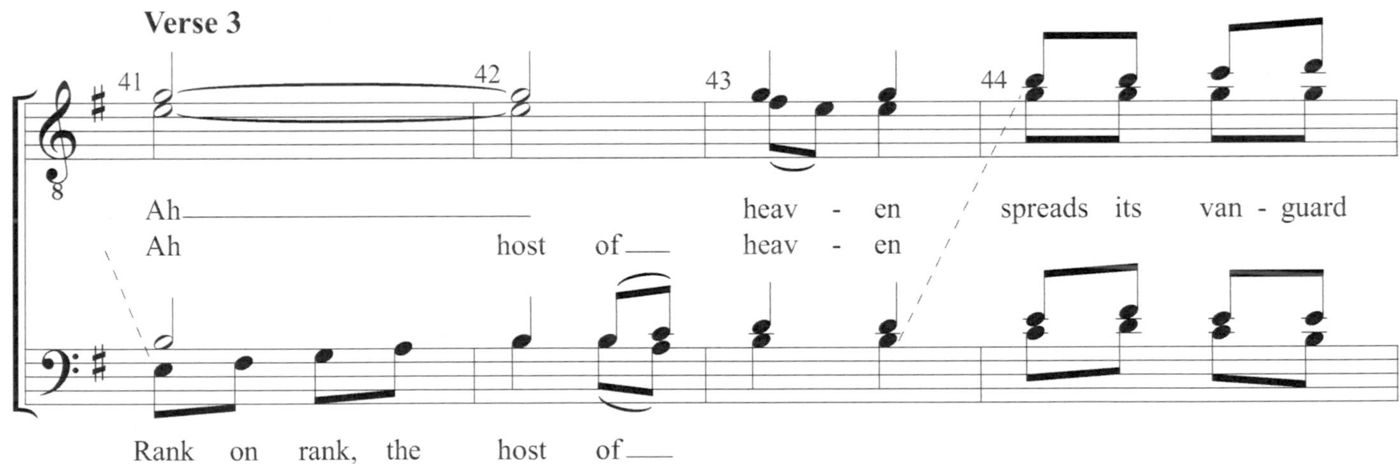
Ah heav - en spreads its van - guard
Ah host of heav - en
Rank on rank, the host of

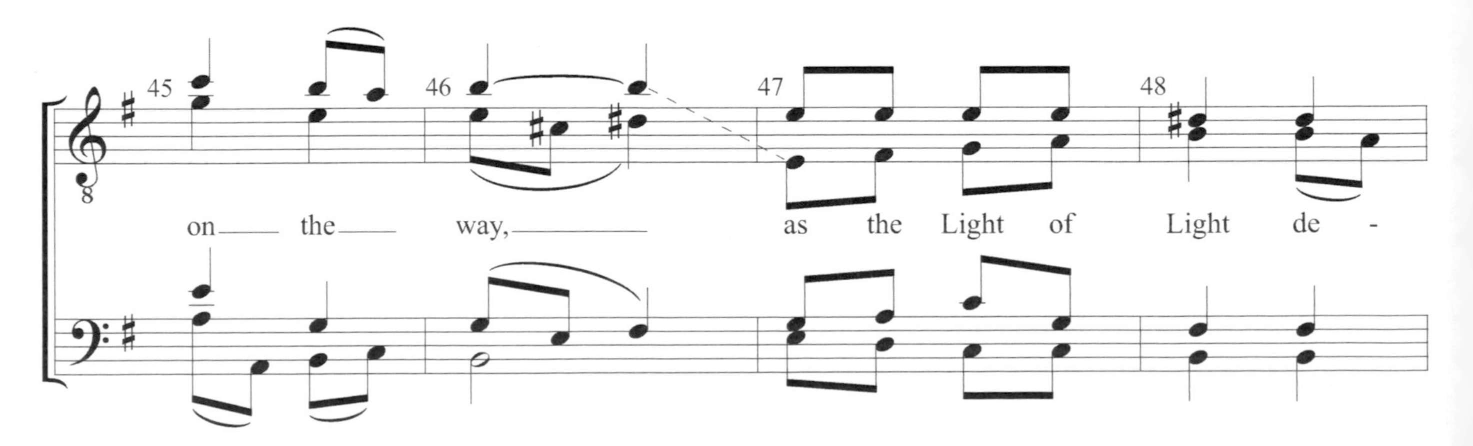
on the way, as the Light of Light de -

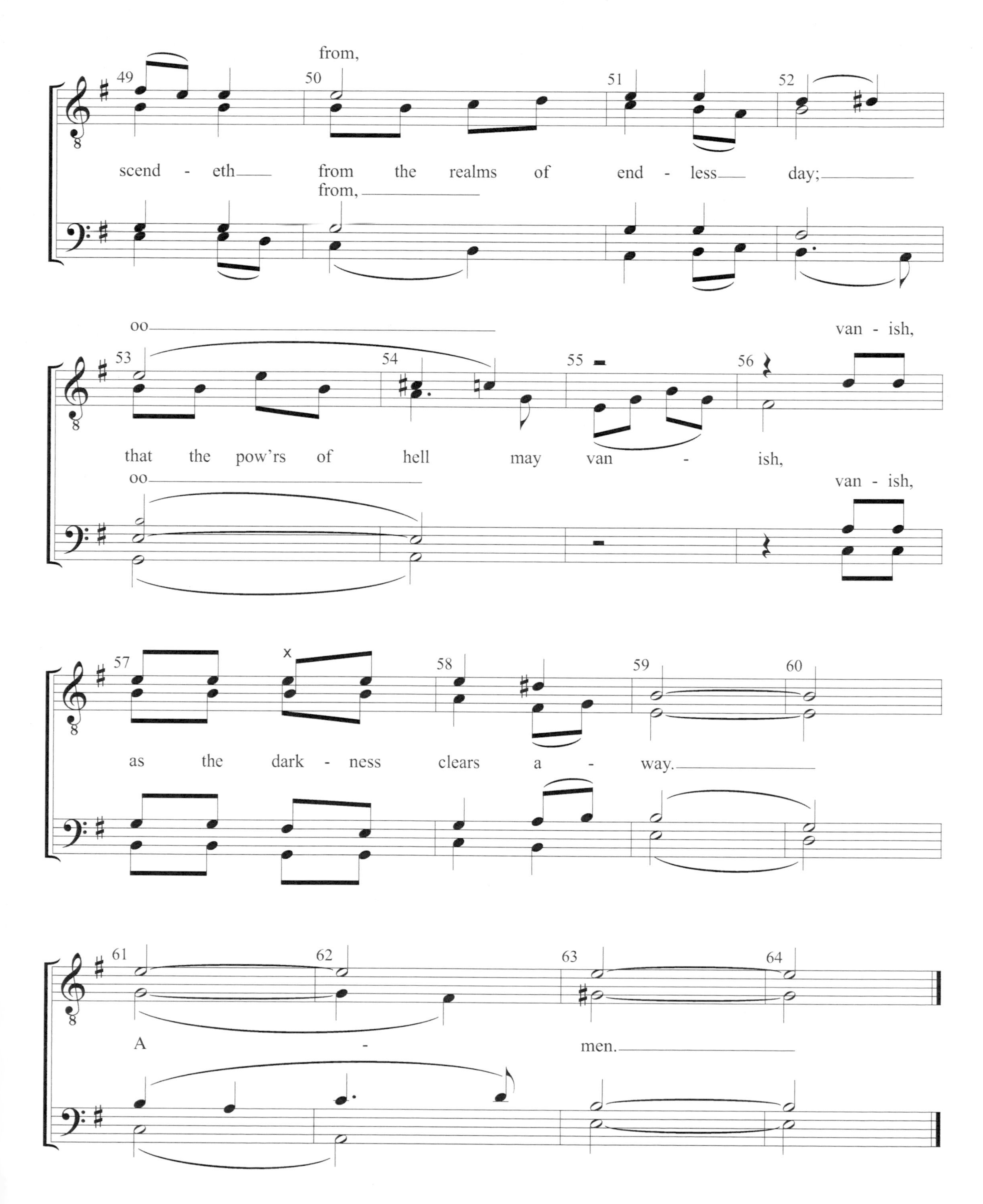
from,
scend - eth from the realms of end - less day;
from,
oo
van - ish,
that the pow'rs of hell may van - ish,
oo
van - ish,
as the dark - ness clears a - way.
A - men.

# AULD LANG SYNE

**(1788)**

Words by ROBERT BURNS

Traditional Scottish Melody
*Arranged by Don Gray*

13 14 15 16
syne, we'll take a cup of kind - ness yet, for — days of auld lang
auld lang syne,
syne,

Reprise
17 18 19 20
syne! For auld — lang — syne, my dear, for auld — lang —

21 22 23
syne, we'll take a cup of kind - ness yet, for
auld lang syne,
syne,

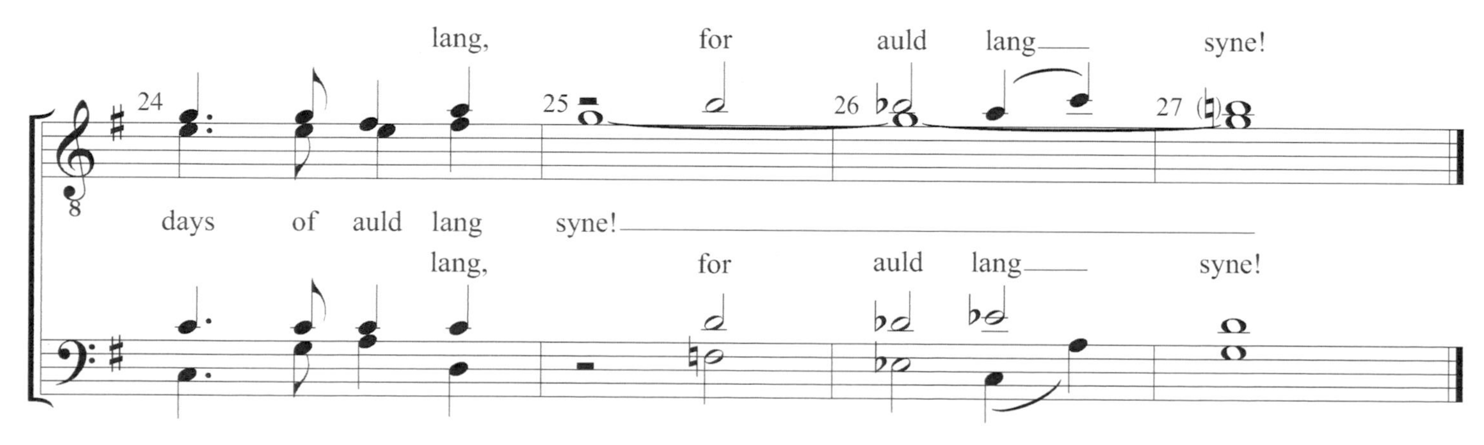
lang, for auld lang — syne!
24 25 26 27
days of auld lang syne! —
lang, for auld lang — syne!

# CHANUKAH, CHANUKAH

Traditional Jewish Carol
*Arranged by Greg Lyne*

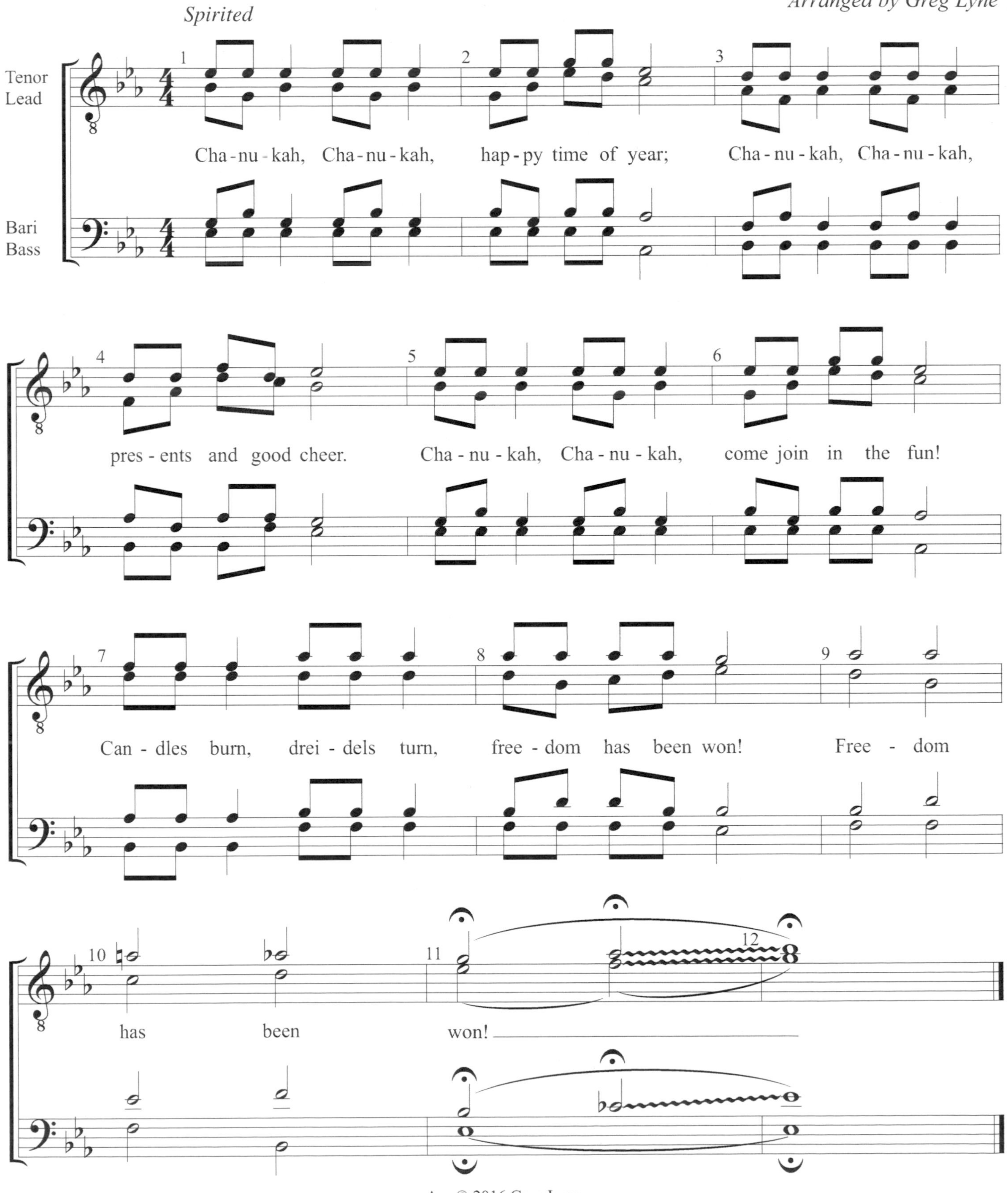